HUNDREDS OF REFLECTIONS

ALSO BY KIRK ADAMS

Left on Paradise

The Electronic Mother

The Trouble with Girls

Husbandry

Measures of Insight: Moral Reflections for Daily Life

HUNDREDS OF REFLECTIONS

100 Psalms Explored in 100 Words

KIRK ADAMS

Kirk Adams Books

Hundreds of Reflections: 100 Psalms Explored in 100 Words

Copyright 2021 by Kirk Adams

All rights reserved, including the right to reproduce this book, or portions thereof, in any form without the press written permission of the publisher except for the use of brief quotations in a book review.

This book was published in the United States of America

Revised Edition (July 2023)

ISBN 978-1-7356062-9-3 (paperback)

ISBN 978-1-7356062-7-9 (ebook)

Kirk Adams Books, PMB #219

45591 Dulles East Plaza, Suite 132

Sterling, VA 20166

"Scripture quotations are from the ESV® Bible (The Holy Bible, English Standard Version®), copyright © 2001 by Crossway, a publishing ministry of Good News Publishers. Used by permission. All rights reserved."

Cover: Peeter Neeffs the Elder, *Antwerp Cathedral* (1656/1561). Courtesy National Gallery of Art, Washington. The National Gallery of Art did not endorse, approve, or participate in the making of this book.

❦ Created with Vellum

To the many who have taught me piety and faith—
even when I have been
an unwilling listener and poor student.

PREFACE

There are plenty of books on the Psalms, so why one more—and this one by a trained historian rather than a theologian? The easy answer would be to reply I am publishing this short book for the instruction of my own children, securing several years of work for their spiritual benefit. A more complete answer would be to note how my doctorate in European history and broad life experiences have convinced me the biblical religion is founded on presuppositions and principles so critical for understanding its meaning that modern readers must dig deeper than what is found in contemporary translations or during cursory searches of the Internet. We must review the Psalms both for what they explicitly state and what they necessarily imply. Often, we must step back into a world very different from our own to contextualize what is being said.

However, I do not want to waste the reader's time and patience with lengthy essays and wordy explanations in a field where I am no expert. To that end, I have arbitrarily limited myself to short expositions of passages from the book of Psalms: 100 passages explored in exactly 100 words each. This self-imposed restriction may be something of an experiment for biblical textual analysis, but is common enough with various communications that frame our lives. Nearly every advertisement from television, radio, and the Internet conveys its message in a few words. Political campaigns, for instance, face strict time limits to make their primary message evident—and so do news headlines, advertising jingles, and even popular songs. This approach also prevents me from talking too much (which I am predisposed to do).

Because this sufficient and efficient approach seems useful, I will attempt here to review short passages from various psalms as the basis for exploring fundamental presuppositions and intrinsic meaning that underpins those passages, especially when considered in historical and comparative religious context. I am neither an Old Testament scholar nor a Hebrew linguist, so I will not delve into the precise translations of ancient languages or the specific cultural context of each particular verse. What I will do is to look across generations and cultures to frame biblical texts in broader context than the narrow limits of a modernity which has grown doctrinaire and shrill. Scholars and readers better educated in Hebrew language and culture will be free to correct or otherwise improve what I have written.

Of course, there can be no doubt the selection of content for my effort represents the types of problems and concerns which I myself have struggled through during my forty-five years of Christian faith and sixty years of human life. What I hope is that the breadth of my experiences has given me a mature (and balanced) approach to Scripture. What I pray is that I have not despised the Word of God as a malleable form into which I have poured my own preferences and prejudices. After all, Christ is quite plain regarding the judgment to fall on anyone and everyone who does so, particularly those who presume to be teachers. While I offer the following thoughts as a means to helping my reader avoid the blinders of today's fashion, I pray that I have not replaced modern errors with my own.

I freely acknowledge my debt to historians such as J.H. Hexter, Herbert Butterfield, and Christopher Dawson (whose writings taught me how to look for a deeper significance in Hebrew history and Christian civilization), as well as to a myriad of Christian thinkers who shaped my own thinking. Without the latter, I would have been lost from my youth. With them, I rejoice in being one man receiving truth from his fathers to pass to his own heirs, and hoping to prove (at least somewhat) faithful in the process. I am particularly indebted to C.S. Lewis—whose influence permeates every page of this book, to include this brief preface. May the Lord repay believing men and women of all generations for the good they have brought to me through their faithful witness.

May the Lord forgive my sins and errors and bless what is good in this book. May Christ also forgive any lack of balance stemming from my hope to discuss a limited set of oft-neglected topics. In particular, I fear my emphasis on the moral righteousness demanded by God throughout the Psalms is insufficiently balanced by a comprehensive examination of God's promise of imputed righteousness as prophesied in the Hebrew sacrificial system and fulfilled in Christ. To that end, I recommend my readers review the works of Martin Luther and John Calvin for passionate and systematic examinations of the doctrine of justification by faith. No man, woman, or child can approach God except through righteousness, but no sinner (which includes each and every one of us) will come to such saving righteousness except through the finished work of Jesus Christ.

My final word of gratitude goes to Uncle Bruce, who spoke kindly to my wife of an earlier draft of this book prior to his passing beyond this life—with a death, I might add, that testified to his life of faith. Remembrance of Bruce's words contributed to my subsequent decision to publish this work, though he is not responsible for any of its faults and flaws.

May the Lord reveal himself anew amidst our unhappy and lost generation, calling many to his goodness and glory.

Kirk Adams

HUNDREDS OF REFLECTIONS

Psalm 1:1. Blessed is the man.

Like creation itself, the book of Psalms begins with *blessing*: a notion rooted in the belief that good (both spiritual and natural) comes only from God's kind disposition. Where happiness is believed to come from good fortune or good luck, men also talk about misfortune and bad luck, but never about what we call *blessing*. But where men understand that God made the world for moral and beneficent purposes, they describe the relationship of divine goodness to human life with a word that reveals both the goodness of God who *blesses* and the grateful dependence of those who are *blessed*.

Psalm 2:1. Why do the nations rage and the peoples plot in vain?

It is striking how separated biblical religion is from the superstition of the ancient world. Nowhere does Scripture declare the gods of Greece or Egypt to possess effective power; the Bible claims only that God exercises authority they do not. Incidents of supernatural activity are rare and entire generations passed without miracle or angelic appearance. Pious Israelites did not plead for deliverance from the evil eye or witch's curse, but from the raging of human enemies—domestic and foreign—believed to be the instruments of evil. Scripture curses the potentate who uses his power to effect false religion and oppression.

PSALM 4:1. Answer me when I call to you, O God of my righteousness! You have given me relief when I was in distress. Be gracious to me and hear my prayer!

Prayers and hymns make no sense unless each man and woman has been created to know God. That is, the Lord is neither a force nor an idea, but a person whose righteous character every human trait should reflect. Israel was called to demonstrate how divinity is one rather than many. Modern believers are called to reveal that divinity is more enduring than mortal life. All believers are called to show God's goodness. The simplest song and most profound prayer alike are predicated on understanding that God exists, has a moral essence, listens to sinners, and cares for individual people.

Psalm 5:11-12. Spread your protection over them, that those who love your name may exult in you. For you bless the righteous, O Lord.

Many turn to talismans and incantations for protection, or to ritual and rite. The Lord would have us turn only to himself since he alone rules human history. What this means is that morality (which is a mirror reflecting God's character) is our foremost concern. Though God loves all people, he distinguishes between those who willingly resemble his goodness and those who do not. No ritual or incantation can save from his displeasure those who divorce themselves from his eternal love and no hex or curse can harm those who do right. Witch hunters wrongly trust spells rather than God.

Psalm 6:1. O Lord, rebuke me not in your anger, nor discipline me in your wrath.

There is an underlying message throughout the psalms not only that the Lord exists and human morality reflects his divine character, but also that the attainment of morality is the supreme human good—far greater than the pursuit and acquisition of power, prestige, or pleasure. That God governs human affairs and disciplines sin like an old-fashioned parent is both acknowledged and praised on the grounds that mankind is in need of moral transformation. We ask only that the Lord be merciful (since we are prone to error and selfishness) as we beg forbearance, lest his blameless character spell our ruin.

Psalm 7:10-11. My shield is with God, who saves the upright in heart. God is a righteous judge, and a God who feels indignation every day.

God's law brings life for the simple reason that the Lord himself governs human history: protecting those who trust him enough to do good and punishing, even to death, those who despise his blameless character by clinging to wrong. It is true that we ought to do good as a philosophical abstraction or moral imperative. Rather, we should do good because such is life itself. Not only do God's laws bring natural good to the flow of human history, but they also cause the Lord to bless or curse as appropriate. Old and New Testament alike reveal this fundamental truth.

Psalm 8:2. Out of the mouths of babies and infants, you have established strength because of your foes, to still the enemy and the avenger.

It is not in negation that we find God. The Lord created the world from nothing so that we might exist and he has no desire for us to meditate on non-existence or otherwise flee reality. For this reason, our souls must not seek existence beyond the physical order, but should be thankful for our place in this natural world. That is, the proper response to creation is not an empty mind, but a grateful heart that adds poems and songs to human life. Since it is God who grants each life, mankind is called to praise his beneficent goodness.

PSALM 9:3. When my enemies turn back, they stumble and perish before your presence.

David's prayers for vindication can appear petulant and self-justifying when considered without context. For instance, when David rejoices in triumph over his enemies, he was speaking of battles that would have taken either his life or that of his foe. At the same time, we must remember how David prayed for enemies, accepted mistreatment from subordinates, and spurned unjust violence. Despite his authority, he was a man with a kind disposition and forgiving attitude: facts we must remember when reflecting on passages in which David praises God for defeating treacherous tribesmen to whom he himself frequently turned the other cheek.

PSALM 10:4. In the pride of his face the wicked does not seek him; all his thoughts are, "There is no God."

The wicked man ignores family and friend as he claws to success. He establishes governments that separate divine goodness from public policy, even turning the life-giving womb into a death-hiding tomb. He posits philosophy and science that leave no room for divinity in God's own creation and accepts how the ruthless inflict suffering on the weak.

From the guillotines of 1793 to the Gulag initiated in 1917 to the horrors uncovered at Auschwitz in 1945, it has been men (and women) whose thoughts, laws, and lives leave no room for God, not the least concern for morality, who massacre multitudes.

※

PSALM 12:3-4. May the Lord cut off all flattering lips, the tongue that makes great boasts, those who say, "With our tongue we will prevail, our lips are with us; who is master over us?

It is unreasonable to expect governments to finance the armies of their mortal foes or communities to empower criminals who rob them. Likewise, God cannot be expected to subsidize those who both rebel against him and persecute his faithful servants. If he sustains human life as Christians believe, there must come a time when the Lord no longer allows evil to usurp his government of the universe. Otherwise, he who is infinite and unchangeable righteousness would stand guilty of material support to selfishness and sin. God's response seems tailored to taking from men the gifts they abuse, including life itself.

※

PSALM 15:1. O Lord, who shall sojourn in your tent? Who shall dwell on your holy hill?

Some psalms undoubtedly were composed in Solomon's temple while others were inspired by Israel's rugged hills. The one universal truth for every psalm is the supplicant's belief that he had encountered God in a way that merited remembrance and emulation. Posture of prayer and sanctity of site mattered far less than spiritual intent since God is known in the heart and mind—in the soul of man wherever a man might be and however he might righteously pray. That is, the Lord is near to those who call him, whether they are in a quiet sanctuary or a noisy throng.

PSALM 18:21. For I have kept the ways of the LORD, and have not wickedly departed from my God.

The ancient world was filled with talismans, spells, magic, astrology, superstition, omens, signs, wonders, and all sorts of mythical beings not observable in the natural order. While Scripture includes some perplexing passages regarding the supernatural, it generally makes clear the main dilemma for mankind is not manipulation of an unseen world of gods and magic, but attainment of moral goodness as a means of acquiring God's favor. The psalms reflect the heart of godliness and include not one word of superstition. Rather, they make evident that the spiritual plague which ails humanity is the moral frailty that corrupts every heart.

PSALM 19:7. The law of the LORD is perfect, reviving the soul; the testimony of the LORD is sure, making wise the simple.

When a man truly delights in God's wisdom and law—not in perfunctory obedience, but from the heart like this psalmist does—then he himself becomes God's creative work in the world and his life is filled with peace: rejoicing in being out of fashion regarding sin and mourning for those who forsake God's good paths. This man puts no political cause or party above piety and willingly faces rejection by family and friend, if need be, for true religion. Not so the man who glues his own judgment to biblical texts or cuts away divine truth as with scissors.

Psalm 20:6. Now I know that the LORD saves his anointed; he will answer him from his holy heaven with the saving might of his right hand.

It should not be thought that the Lord's promise to hear prayer means that every petition will be granted. While David asks God to give to the godly the desires of their heart, he did not hope for lustful and envious wishes to be realized, but observes how God listens from heaven: a realm of moral perfection in which no base thing or illegitimate petition is considered. As for unanswered prayer, David suffered sorrow throughout his life and petitioned the Lord with seemingly unanswered prayers preceding the deaths of two sons: the newborn child of Bathsheba and the traitor Absalom.

Psalm 22:17. I can count all my bones—they stare and gloat over me.

Because the gospels draw from this psalm to portray Jesus as promised Messiah, this passage requires us to make a decision regarding a prophet who lived one thousand years after David lamented these sorrows. But we also must consider this psalm in context of David's own troubles, noting how the psalmist observes the limits often placed on human suffering. That is, during antiquity a broken bone was not easily mended with x-rays and splints. Indeed, fractures could cause disfigurement, impairment, and chronic pain. David here recognizes that even amidst his many terrible troubles, God has saved him from utter ruin.

Psalm 23:1-3. The LORD is my shepherd; I shall not want. He makes me lie down in green pastures.

In reciting this song, we confess that the words of this poet are far more than mere historical statements: utterances used by scholars to contextualize ancient religion. By the simple fact of using the psalm as a guide to prayer (which clearly is the intent of its author), we are confessing that the same God who took care of David's needs and providentially led that ruler through many troubles into a kingdom of righteousness also will guide us through our years and deliver us from our enemies, human and natural. God will use us to build his kingdom on earth.

PSALM 23:4. Even though I walk through the valley of the shadow of death, I will fear no evil ... your rod and your staff, they comfort me.

It is not holy martyrdom that we should seek or desire. It is God who blesses his children with life, protects them from many evils, and calls them to pray for such protection. That is, believers rightly hope that their God will spare them from poverty, shame, ignorance, pain, slavery, and disease. Of course, the inevitability of death makes it clear there is never complete escape from such sorrows (even as this psalmist reveals how the Lord protects us from much grief as we follow him and pray his favor). The resurrection of Jesus is the ultimate triumph over sorrow.

PSALM 24:3. Who shall ascend the hill of the LORD? And who shall stand in his holy place?

Mankind is afraid of divine mysteries. We fear being swallowed by infinity: no longer remembered for who we ourselves are and what we aspire to. While ancient pagan mystery cults drowned the human spirit in dissipation and medieval ascetic fanatics forsook their flesh with self-denial, this psalmist remind us that we ourselves are God's creative work, each of us with our particular attributes of talent and aspiration. Moreover, the psalmist also reveals how God is to be approached not as an unfathomable mystery, but as a divine person—both as limitless as infinity and as indivisible as a single thought.

Psalm 25:8. Good and upright is the LORD; therefore he instructs sinners in the way.

There are several ways by which people justify themselves over God. The first is to be the hypocrite who claims unmerited virtue. The second is to confess wrongdoing while shifting blame to circumstances or society. The third is to take credit for good that God brings into existence. The fourth way is the most dangerous of all: for it is to judge God's moral laws as obsolete or otherwise irrelevant. Anyone who labels eternal truth as unnecessary or outdated stands in judgment of and justifies himself over God. In contrast, the humble acknowledge God's laws and confess their many sins.

Psalm 27:4. One thing have I asked of the LORD ...

One of the more remarkable characteristics possessed by David was his willingness to pray to God time and again, always with hope. He never grew weary of praying to the Lord as trials returned and he never denied God's goodness simply because his own sorrows and suffering proved persistent. Indeed, it was in the cycle of sorrow and deliverance that David developed a faith in the Lord: a faith much stronger for having been proven many times. Just as David faced many foreign and domestic enemies, we too should expect to face persistent troubles in every element of our lives.

Psalm 28:1. To you, O Lord, I call ...

The psalmist undoubtedly participated in ritual sacrifices *to* the Lord and here devotes not the blood of unblemished lambs but the praises of his heart *to* God. This idea of giving anything (sacrificial lambs or psalm alike) *to* the Lord is profound. It presupposes the reality of human free will and of divine benevolence alike: that God so regards us that he demands and blesses our simplest gesture of gratitude. It also presupposes the necessity of ordering priorities rightly, so that the Lord is at the center of ritual and spontaneous prayer alike. All of our life belongs *to* God.

Psalm 31:10-11. For my life is spent with sorrow, and my years with sighing; my strength fails because of my iniquity, and my bones waste away ... I have become a reproach ... and an object of dread to my acquaintances.

As we listen to the psalmist, two points become clear. First, nature is real and the pious man remains subject to every human emotion (including depression, anxiety, and sorrow) in the midst of his piety. That is, we must not expect faith to shield us from human sadness and worry. Second, as we observe family and friend suffer calamity and grief, we must be careful not to censure. Some of them may be like the pious psalmist (namely David) who suffered for his righteousness after God called him to become warrior and ruler. Not every sorrow or shame is self-induced.

Psalm 32:3. For when I kept silent, my bones wasted away ...

This psalm rightly is understood as a hymn of repentance. It less often is appreciated that this psalm, along with every psalm or hymn ever written, reveals the need that mankind has to speak to God. Far from being an unfounded myth, the biblical account of mankind in paradise is fully consistent with the observed human need to communicate with God: to pray to our Creator and to be heard by him. We must not understand reality only from within ourselves, but must cry out to God in prayer and praise. Indeed, we suffer when we refuse to do so.

Psalm 33:1. Shout for joy in the LORD, O you righteous! Praise befits the upright.

It is necessary that those who worship God be morally upright and that those who are morally upright worship God. The Lord who makes mankind would not have us hide evil behind faith. Religion that harms neighbors or plots against enemies is blasphemous since God would have his people do good to everyone. Moreover, it also is necessary for those who live piously to acknowledge God as the giver of all good—and not they themselves. With such praise we acknowledge that the determination of right and power of righteousness comes from God rather than from parents, politics, or philosophy.

※

PSALM 34:1. I will bless the LORD at all times; his praise shall continually be in my mouth.

When I was younger, I misunderstood the instruction to *always* be filled with the Spirit and was oppressed by my desire to displace ordinary human existence with hyper-spirituality. I failed to realize that God had made creation separate from himself for the deliberate purpose of making a good universe distinct from divinity. I also failed to realize that (because Scripture sometimes uses language prosaically or poetically) pedantic interpretations can mislead. Even as this particular author tells us that he *continually* extols God, he himself is thinking about the people for whom he is composing this song (not only about God).

※

PSALM 37:10-11. In just a little while, the wicked will be no more ... the meek shall inherit the land.

In the Sermon on the Mount, Christ promised that the meek would inherit the earth, plainly drawing on the prayer of this psalmist—and the moral and prophetic utterances upon which the psalmist based his prayer. The triumph of the meek (those who are innocent and lowly) cannot be separated from triumph over evil. God will not merely exalt slaves over masters or workers over capitalists, but promises to destroy every form of oppression so that justice overflows with mercy. With all violence, perversion, hypocrisy, and dishonesty (and their practitioners) removed, everything good and honest will prosper in the land.

PSALM 39:13. Look away from me, that I may smile again, before I depart and am no more!

A theme runs through Scripture, from the lives of the patriarchs to the parables of Christ (and apostolic theology), that men dare not justify themselves before God. They cannot legitimately excuse their selfish choices and callous hearts, and intuitively understand that sin brings and deserves death. Such is our corruption that we do not want God, fellow believers, or even decent people to see who we really are. We cause our own shame and often would rather pretend that God does not exist than to confess ourselves as truly unworthy before him. Moral blight explains why so many hate religion.

PSALM 40:13. Be pleased, O LORD, to deliver me! O LORD, make haste to help me!

Prayer is where we reveal who we believe God to be. Those who portray him as an unfeeling potentate demanding blind obeisance are satisfied to pray with words they do not understand and in languages they have never learned. Those who see him as a mere first cause without influence in their lives form prayers primarily to please their listeners. Still, anyone who believes that God truly cares for the world presents petitions before him knowing that he will work all things for the good of everyone who asks, whether his answer to a particular request is yes or no.

❧

Psalm 41:13. Blessed be the LORD, the God of Israel, from everlasting to everlasting! Amen and Amen.

The matter is quite simple: either God is real and those who deny the reality of divinity explain away the dictates of their own hearts or else religious believers bow before idolatrous notions of divinity just as ridiculous as was the worship of pagan gods made from plaster and stone. If God exists, it is those who imagine that the universe sprang from absolutely nothing, or otherwise existed eternally, who are blindly superstitious since their cosmology is at odds with their science and philosophy—which ultimately deny that the cosmos can bring itself into being or exist endlessly without beginning.

❧

Psalm 42: 1. As a deer pants for flowing streams, so pants my soul for you, O God.

Understanding the Psalms (or any Scripture) presupposes a clean heart. Indeed, it is the same for any type of human learning. The diligent student learns his math formulas better than the lazy one and the prudent politician foresees danger better than the corrupt one. This is to say that human beings can change and mature only when we want to (even our bodies grow strong only when we choose to eat). Mankind must desire God with heart and soul to find him, and we will not find him when we only go through motions or refuse to repent our sins.

※

PSALM 44:1. O God, we have heard with our ears, our fathers have told us, what deeds you performed in their days, in the days of old.

Human testimony is so valuable that true religion insists men and women should listen to those who came before them and pass to their own children what they have heard of God's acts in human history. Pagan myths were rooted not in particular places and times, but in timeless tales and epic poems. In contrast, God's revelation states that mankind should believe only credible accounts which have been confirmed by trustworthy witnesses and for which there are public records and testimony by unbiased observers. It is the liar and deceiver who claims divine visions that only he himself has seen.

※

PSALM 47:1. Clap your hands, all peoples! Shout to God with loud songs of joy!

If Scripture is God-breathed, then the Lord has caused this psalmist to sing praises to himself. While those who do not know God's triune and infinite nature may rebel against the idea that God causes his own praises to be sung, those who know how supremely good God is will rejoice that he has opened their eyes to divine perfection. Indeed, by calling men to worship himself, God helps us to become better people—just as our parents made us grow in morals and manners whenever they required us to recognize their support, honor their love, and express our gratitude.

※

Psalm 49:3-4. My mouth shall speak wisdom ... I will solve my riddle to the music of the lyre.

Psalms cannot be understood in isolation. They reflect the heart of biblical religion, but by themselves would provide only a vapid sentimentality with little substance. The Lord never intended to separate psalm singing from holy living. Before the psalms were given, Israel first was called into existence and subsequently provided the laws of Moses. In this psalm, we see that wisdom itself is found in the mind of the psalmist as he drafts his song. That is, worship of God involves remembering his righteous laws, profound goodness, and providential care. Anyone who separates God's praise from holy living does wrong.

※

Psalm 49:10. For he sees that even the wise die; the fool and the stupid alike must perish and leave their wealth to others.

Praise of God should not begin with emotions and enthusiasm or draw its strength primarily through harp and violin, but must flow from moral reasoning. Only after we have examined facts of spirit and nature are we able to frame appropriate spiritual responses to our lives: rejoicing in the good and beautiful and denouncing the evil and ugly. Such songs exclude nonsense lyrics and include intelligible ideas that reveal righteousness. Indeed, the observations on which our songs and prayers are based are the possession of all mankind and reveal how God's religion lights the path into wisdom that brings life.

※

PSALM 50:5, 23. "Gather to me my faithful [one]... who offers thanksgiving as his sacrifice glorifies me.

Sacrifice is not waste, but a reckoning that God really exists. If God were a projection or an ideological opiate, our sermons would be his lifeblood—his effective cause—like pagan sacrifices were believed to feed their gods. Our offerings would be the sustenance to support ministers motivated to preach religion in exchange for easy jobs. No, the Lord calls us to burn our offerings precisely because he truly exists in himself and needs nothing from us. Sacrifice allows us to burn bridges before mankind to demonstrate that we do not secretly believe more in mortal accomplishments than in God.

※

PSALM 51. A Psalm of David, when Nathan the Prophet went to him, after he had gone to Bathsheba.

We must be careful not to be excessively harsh with our religious leaders when they prove to be sinful. David wrote religious songs, represented faith in Israel, and was made king for his fervent piety, yet also lusted for the wife of one of his military officers—impregnating the woman and subsequently scheming to have her husband killed during battle. Though sin does not get much worse than that, David's eventual repentance reveals how God forgives sin and cleanses the corruption of those repent before him rather than to justify their misconduct or explain away God's existence and moral commands.

PSALM 53:1. The fool says in his heart, "There is no God."

This passage makes clear that many people deny God's existence because they participate in moral crime and would rather obstruct justice than confess guilt. We all have heard ridiculous tales told by children trying to hide misbehavior and stupid stories from accused criminals attempting to trick judges and deceive juries. This psalmist confesses the moral corruption of mankind, himself included, and is able to repent his faults and change his ways like a child or criminal coming clean. But he who will not admit his moral turpitude inevitably challenges the reality of sin, the divine law, and God's very existence.

PSALM 55:7-8. I would wander far away; I would lodge in the wilderness ... to find a shelter from the raging wind and tempest.

It is necessary to handle Scripture with care. While Jesus taught that every fallen sparrow is regarded by our Father in heaven, Christ's teaching is not a call to adopt stoic philosophy, but to trust in God's goodness. Here we see the psalmist (whose every word is divinely inspired) protest that his suffering is so terrible that he would flee to the desert, far from the storm, if he could do so. In the same spirit, we must never declare, or otherwise pretend, that the sorrows of life are not painful. The Lord calls us to be troubled by troubles.

※

Psalm 58:10. The righteous will rejoice when he sees the vengeance; he will bathe his feet in the blood of the wicked.

Without doubt, this is the most terrifying passage of Scripture. While some fall away on account of it or explain away the prophecy as Hebrew hyperbole and primitive religion, it seems to me that the passage speaks a comforting thought with unvarnished frankness. Are we really horrified that Russian soldiers poked the burned bones of Hitler? Do we not rejoice that the perpetrators of the Holocaust were captured, tried, and executed? Are we not thankful for bloody battles won against cruel oppressors? This passage reminds us that the victim himself will experience God's avenging answer to prayers uttered during persecution.

※

Psalm 58:10. [The righteous] will bathe his feet in the blood of the wicked.

Translations matter. The psalmist is not talking about wallowing in bloodthirsty vengeance, but uses a verb elsewhere translated as *washing* (i.e. one's hands in innocence). Like my word *wallowing*—which has a physical sense along with a moral meaning—this *bathing* speaks more of soul than body, even as it signifies ancient soldiers splashing through spilled blood in spear and sword warfare. A modern equivalent might paraphrase "*the godly will be splattered by the blood of the foe*"—an expression denoting both the triumph of the just and the sufferings of war. The victory of the just is taught here.

Psalm 61:5. *You have given me the heritage of those who fear your name.*

Perhaps the most obvious and least noted feature of the psalms is that they were written by living people. That is, a young man who dies in a drunken accident will not write a psalm in maturity and a girl rendered infertile through promiscuity will not become the mother to a daughter who will sing psalms. Scripture everywhere reminds us that God gives life (including a good heritage) to those who serve him and humbles those who make war against him. If we desire God's blessing so that our children and grandchildren are blessed, we must serve him whole-heartedly today.

Psalm 66:18. If I had cherished iniquity in my heart, the Lord would not have listened.

Even if we offer public worship, God will not be pleased if we refuse him what he demands: ourselves. This unyielding insistence is not divine intolerance, but the desire of Infinite Love to live in our very selves. That is, God does not dwell in cathedrals and temples made of mortar and stone, but offers to bless every person with an indwelling of divine life to welcome each of us into an inheritance of eternal joy. Thankfully, the Lord knows our weakness as he forgives and forbears much sin, demanding only that we cherish his goodness over rivals and idols.

Psalm 68:6. God settles the solitary in a home; he leads out the prisoners to prosperity, but the rebellious dwell in a parched land.

There are two ways to consider how God answers prayer. The first is to consider specific interventions such as miraculous healings or implausible acts of Providence. Such interventions are rare and few will experience them, now or in the past. The second is to remember the life-long leading of God to redeem his people: to save them from moral blindness and lonely despair, as well as from legal shackles and political persecution. All of us are required to acknowledge what the Lord has done in our lives by redeeming us from our sins and by saving us from sinful men.

Psalm 69:2. I sink in deep mire, where there is no foothold.

There are situations and circumstances too difficult to accept and too complex to understand. Often, human beings are so blinded by family quarrels, political struggles, or ecclesiastical schism that we are rendered unable to identify root causes, offer solutions, or heal divisions. Sometimes, we cannot even begin to sort out such problems, but must observe the hardening attitudes of those with whom we must deal. At such times, we should understand that a callous heart filled with bitterness and self-justification can no more come from the Lord than a submissive and humble spirit can rise from defiance of God's Word.

Psalm 69:4. More in number than the hairs of my head are those who hate me without cause ... What I did not steal must I now restore?

Faith is tested in the conscience: in a person's willingness to do what is right despite conflicting passions. It also is tested as human beings (born of parents to live among people) dwell among family, friends, and compatriots. Those who do right inevitably face opposition from those who do wrong, and natural ties cannot prevent persecutions. Moreover, godly people often are despised by those whose consciences are hardened by the unflinching demands of morality and who consequently subject the pious to persecution, sniping, and slander. Jesus possibly remembered this psalm when teaching that God numbered every hair on our heads.

PSALM 71:4. Rescue me, O my God, from the hand of the wicked, from the grasp of the unjust and cruel man.

Scripture does not promise that God will perform miracles or send providential signs to prove his existence. What it promises is that God will be with his people to overcome their enemies. While the Lord's people may suffer calamity as judgment for sin or individual Christians may be sorely tested through suffering, the Bible declares that ultimately God will deliver his people from the hand of their foe. Anyone who calls to the Lord can struggle and suffer in confidence that the gates of hell will not prevail against God's work. Triumph is certain, both on earth and in heaven.

PSALM 73:13. All in vain have I kept my heart clean and washed my hands in innocence.

There is little doubt that the human heart is self-deceiving and that we must accept Christ's judgments regarding the flaws found in human nature. Still, this psalmist is moved by God to declare how he was motivated by moral uprightness. That is, while Scripture never lets human beings pretend to be more righteousness than they really are, it also teaches that God separates right from wrong in the human heart just as he once made creation from absolutely nothing. It is materialists and atheists who cynically believe humanity motivated solely by narcissistic self-love, unconscious sexual impulses, and deterministic economic interests.

PSALM 73:21-22. When my soul was embittered, when I was pricked in heart, I was brutish and ignorant; I was like a beast toward you.

Piety is not consistent with an unthinking existence. From patriarch to apostle, Scripture reveals how true piety requires contemplation and self-examination. Even suffering must not be allowed to blind us to what is true. It is the materialist who believes that the world and its ideals emanate from physics and biology; the believer understands that the creation itself was conceived in the eternal deliberation of divine goodness. For that reason, the Bible insists that mankind not imitate unreasoning and amoral animals: senseless and brutish in the face of good and evil. Philosopher or not, we are called to contemplate eternity.

PSALM 77:3. When I remember you, God ...

We know God from memory, not through intuition or direct encounter. We learn of his past deeds and project from them what he will do in the future. That is why Scripture must be without error when it records God's work among his people. It is why we honor what God has done in our lives by showing gratitude that he redeems our souls and directs our steps. That is, because God values truth, meditation, and gratitude (and we are made like him), his servants must have accurate memories as they recount their stories, honor their ancestors, and interpret history.

❦

PSALM 78:1. O my people, hear my teaching: listen to the words of my mouth.

At the core of the psalms is the notion that God speaks to us through other people. The biblical religion is not some hidden mystery, but is God's work among human communities. This psalmist confesses that God has inspired one person to write down divinely-authored prayers yo be instructive to others. If God really inspired this psalmist (which would be the only possible justification for reading these ancient songs beyond mere literary curiosity), then the truth is that the Lord has set eternal thoughts into a particular language at a specific time, thereby revealing himself to them and us alike.

❦

PSALM 81:1. [Of Asaph] Sing aloud to God our strength; shout for joy to the God of Jacob!

This psalm mentions Jacob and Asaph, both of them males. Why did God put divine words almost exclusively into the mouths of Jewish men? Why did he not equally entrust prophecy to Jewish women or Gentile converts? The first point to remember is that blessing necessarily involves discrimination: giving to one rather than to another. While the Lord raises every mountain, he makes some higher than others. Second, it should be observed that every great idea or institution was developed by particular men and women rather than rising as an indiscriminate human achievement. That is, aggregated mankind accomplishes very little.

☙❦☙

PSALM 84:11. The LORD bestows favor and honor. No good thing does he withhold from those who walk uprightly.

Our lives come down to this: does God exist and are his promises particular to each person? If so, we may show courage and resolve in facing troubles which rush at us. If not, no amount of confidence or courage will prevent us from being wrecked on life's rocks whenever fate turns against us. It is in this sense that the weakest faith is more effective than the greatest determination of an unbelieving man. Each of us must ask whether it was chance or a gift of God that replaced loneliness with joy, sickness with health, and folly with wisdom.

☙❦☙

PSALM 85:0. To the choirmaster ... of the sons of Korah.

At the heart not only of religion but of life is a question: does good always come from God or can it exist independent of him? This psalm (composed by Hebrew musicians called the Sons of Korah) is a God-breathed writing drafted by and through men. While the notion that God inspired Scripture raises many issues, the main point often is missed: that God, who initially created our world, inspires men to do all sort of good deeds in it. He still makes men to write psalms, teach religion, ponder history, wage war, and raise families—among other good deeds.

❧

Psalm 88:6. You have put me in the depths of the pit, in the regions dark and deep.

Some believe everything created by God is delightful and pleasant. The words of this psalmist teach otherwise. If we believe Scripture to be inspired by God, then the gloom experienced by this author reflects how God calls men to feel during times of sorrow. That is, people suffering great loss are called to express faith in lamentation just as people whose lives are filled with blessing should express their faith with thanksgiving. The Lord is the author of sad sentiment (and sentences) when suffering is endured in a faith resolved to confess that Christ governs every element of his cosmos.

❧

Psalm 89:1. I will sing of the steadfast love of the LORD …

Some perceive a conflict between knowing God and knowing about God—experiential reality versus propositional revelation. This psalm make clear that the point of faith is to know the Lord such that he becomes as real as any other person (in truth, not fantasy) and even more so since he is the cause of all life and truth. Such immediacy in our knowledge of the Lord is best seen when we sing praises to him with joyful hearts in a way that we do not sing to philosophical abstractions and mathematical propositions. We are to know and enjoy God forever.

※

Psalm 91:2. I will say to the LORD, "My refuge and my fortress, my God, in whom I trust."

Before we discuss law and grace or right and wrong, we must address the relationship that stands before every other: that of God to man. Throughout the psalms, the God of Israel is referred to as *Lord,* a title now so banal and absorbed into our sense of benevolent divinity that it paraphrases either as *friend* or *sir* for many modern people—who generally conceive of God as a mannerly gentleman. In ancient Israel, however, the name *lord* was a noble title used in a functioning aristocracy unlimited by modern democratic norms. It denoted power over property, courts, and armies.

※

Psalm 94:8-9. Understand, O dullest of the people! Fools, when will you be wise? He who planted the ear, does he not hear? He who formed the eye, does he not see?

At its core, the biblical religion rises from two simple maxims. First, it is impossible to believe that the universe is self-created. Second, there is a difference between good and evil. Anyone who accepts these propositions necessarily accepts the existence of a Creator who transcends mortality and upholds morality, rewarding good and punishing evil. Everyone who denies these principles is required to explain how the universe is eternally existent or self-created from absolutely nothing. They also must deny that horrors like the Holocaust are morally evil on the indisputable grounds that moral categories do not exist in an amoral universe.

※

PSALM 99:6. Moses and Aaron were among his priests, Samuel also was among those who called upon his name. They called to the LORD, and he answered them.

While Scripture asserts its historicity and reliability, making clear that its miracles and stories are accurate narratives, it does so in context of emphasizing our need to choose for God as our spiritual forefathers did. Like the ancients, we face the decision whether to hold fast to the supreme good or to surrender ourselves to transient pleasures. And just as our forefathers chose without understanding everything God later would reveal, so also we cannot have every question about Scripture answered before we choose. Even modern scientists must choose how they should live, though they cannot explain how their lives originated.

※

PSALM 100:3. Know that the LORD, he is God! It is he who made us, and we are his; we are his people, and the sheep of his pasture.

This psalm is a waste of time if the Lord does not exist. Some might find value in shared religious emotions and sentiment, but I do not. If the Lord is no more real than pagan gods were, then prayers made in his name are of no more value than pagan rituals once were: mere manipulation and superstition. But if the Lord really exists, then our every thought and deed ought to conform to his good character and we can live our lives with the quiet confidence that this psalmist expresses in rejoicing how God takes cares of his people.

※

PSALM 103:13-15. As a father shows compassion to his children, so the LORD shows compassion to those who fear him ... As for man, his days are like grass; he flourishes like a flower of the field.

We must never forget that Scripture is the source of Jesus's teaching. Indeed, two passages from the Sermon on the Mount seem rooted in this psalm: the notion that God loves mankind even more than parents love their children and the belief that mankind ultimately is dependent on God rather than mere nature. Though we are unable to explain exactly how Jesus composed his thoughts, we can see in this psalm where he rooted his teachings. And if we are to imitate Christ by being filled with God's Spirit, we must imitate how Jesus understood and subordinated himself to Scripture.

※

PSALM 104:2-3. You are clothed with splendor and majesty, covering yourself with light as with a garment, stretching out the heavens like a tent.

The Lord uses the language of poetry rather than of science or philosophy to reveal his divine nature. Words such as *infinite* and *eternal,* while useful for philosophical analysis, can make God seem abstract and unapproachable. Not so the poetic language chosen by the prophets in which God's unlimited nature and divine character are presented such that Almighty God in some sense seems accessible. If it is idolatrous to encapsulate divinity in stone gods, then it is unreasonable to define God as an impersonal force with less soul than we possess—less able than mankind to think, feel, and choose.

PSALM 104:15. [God makes] wine to gladden the heart of man, oil to make his face shine and bread to strengthen man's heart.

If Scripture reveals God as Christians believe, then we must subordinate ourselves not simply to its explicit commands, but also to its perceptions and perspectives. In this instance, we must remember that the Bible neither provides an ascetic's rule of discipline which denies the value of ordinary life nor denigrates the natural realm created by God. Indeed, Scripture teaches that it is God who places value on wine that brings mirth, oil that brings beauty, and bread that brings strength. While these gifts must never be preferred over faith, neither should they intentionally be sacrificed for surliness, ugliness, and weakness.

PSALM 104:24-25. O LORD, how manifold are your works! In wisdom have you made them all; the earth is full of your crea-

tures. Here is the sea, great and wide, which teems with creatures innumerable, living things both small and great.

Scripture is unapologetic in asserting God's reign over a natural realm far great and grander than mankind can ever measure. The fact that there are trillions of stars beyond the already countless multitudes observed in the night skies over ancient Israel would not have troubled this psalmist. Nor would he have been bothered by modern discoveries regarding life hidden in the ocean depths. Unlike early modern astronomers overwhelmed to discover that the cosmos was greater than pagan philosophers comprehended, this psalmist starts with praise of a Milky Way unobscured by modern lighting and a Mediterranean sea undiminished by commercial fishing.

※

PSALM 107:9. For he satisfies the longing soul ... the hungry soul he fills with good things.

When a man thanks God for his daily bread, he makes an idol of himself if he secretly believes that he alone is responsible for securing his work and procuring his wage (as in an old movie when a character blessed his meal in God's name while complaining that he did the work himself and failed to understand how God had contributed anything). If we are to avoid self-idolatry and doubtful prayers, we must understand that God governs his world and provides for us. That is, the simplest prayer requires theological, historical, and scientific insight if it will glorify God.

PSALM 107:10-13. Some sat in darkness and in the shadow of death, prisoners in affliction and in irons, for they had rebelled against the words of God ... Then they cried to the LORD in their trouble, and he delivered them from their distress.

We must not miss the point of conversion. To turn to the Lord is not to accept him like a pagan amulet or incantation: something not really understood, but believed to effect miracles or cures. No, to turn to the Lord is to realize we have done wrong, repent of particular sins, and ask that the Lord forgive wrongs we cannot erase. This process affirms that God's moral perfections ought to be the basis of every decision we make, whether as individuals or groups. Done rightly, it also reminds us of our inner corruption and need for God's great mercy.

PSALM 107:33-35. He turns rivers into a desert, springs of water into thirsty ground ... He turns a desert into pools of water, a parched land into springs of water.

Faith is not fantasy. It is neither make-believe nor delusion, but is grounded in God's government of chance and circumstance to benefit everyone who calls on the Lord. Faith believes that the words of God bring contentment and joy far better than do other philosophies (or pursuits) and that chance and coincidence benefit those who serve the Lord. If the spiritual life that God requires does not lead to happiness, God did not make us. If the people of God disappear like the devotees of ancient gods, Christ is not their protector. We are told to assess faith in history.

❦

Psalm 109:14. May the iniquity of his fathers be remembered before the LORD, and let not the sin of his mother be blotted out!

Mere nature suggests that the complaints of the oppressed die with them (except when pursued by others on their behalf) and hints that injustice signifies little. Conscience, however, impresses into us understanding that we must render an accounting for every false word and selfish act—lest morality prove less effectual than nagging. The question is simple: does morality die with humanity? Did the Supreme Good exist prior to the Big Bang? Does human nature necessarily demand both physical existence and moral ideal? The psalmist reveals that God establishes moral truth by blotting out evil through divine control of human affairs.

❦

Psalm 109:22. For I am poor and needy, and my heart is stricken within me.

Because we know ourselves to be corrupt and powerless, we scarcely can accept that the Infinite God can work through our wills and inclinations in the same way he uses inanimate objects. At least part of our difficulty is that we cannot imagine any means of control beyond our own limited power over nature. God, however, does not need arms and legs—or warriors and teachers, for that matter—to cause human actions. His power is at once more direct and less obvious. Remember that he moves mountains not with arms and legs, but through divine decrees and natural laws.

Psalm 112:2. His offspring will be mighty in the land; the generation of the upright will be blessed.

We must remember that the worship of God is conducted amidst human life: family, friend, and field. We are not angelic beings made in heaven, but humans born of earth. Indeed, God so cares for temporal life that he blesses it generation after generation for all who serve him. To be blunt, if you told me that the point of my prayers is to escape temporal life, I would despair; but if you tell me, as this psalmist does, that God is utterly interested in the earthly fate of my still-unconceived grandchildren, I will praise him with all my heart.

Psalm 113:7-9. He raises the poor from the dust and lifts the needy from the ash heap, to make them sit with princes ... He gives the barren woman a home, making her the joyous mother of children.

God's redemption is so great that he includes salvation not merely of disembodied souls in an ethereal heaven, but also deliverance of lost people from dark days. Salvation surely brings the forgiveness of sin for those who repent, but also repair of broken lives for those who allow Christ to remake their souls—as well as the providential care for all who trust him to prove wise and good in his government of human affairs. Everyone has known men of faith raised from humble beginnings to great honor and women led from lonely sorrows to loving marriages and large families.

Psalm 114:1-2. When Israel went out from Egypt, the house of Jacob from a people of strange language ...

Spirituality perfects rather than replaces nature. It often is forgotten that there can be no Scripture without development of a skill that predates prophecy: the ability to read and write. That is, God used literate men born into literate societies as prophets and scribes. The question is why God passed his word through the scroll and book rather than through mystical experience and oral tradition. The answer likely is because the written word is the best means to maintain accuracy and clear expression, which is why it makes no sense to accept Scripture's divine authority if we doubt its accuracy.

Psalm 116:9. I will walk before the LORD in the land of the living. I believed even when I spoke ...

It is not angels who compose holy songs and psalms in Scripture, but men and women made of flesh and blood. While the psalms always remind us of the duties of morality and religion, these songs also come from biblical authors who lived ordinary human lives and spent their days with family, friends, and compatriots just as we do. Indeed, this psalmist explicitly teaches that God's blessing is to give an ordinary life to his servants. True piety is consistent with a normal life, only insisting that God be loved more than creation and that we love neighbors as ourselves.

※

Psalm 119:47. I find my delight in your commandments, which I love.

Throughout the history of the church, there have been various interpretations regarding the relationship of the Old and New Testaments and of the place of moral law in the Christian life. A comparison of this psalm with the first letter of John provides everything we must know to live well. Both this Hebrew song and John's Greek epistle reveal the same teaching: people moved by God have his laws written on their hearts to the extent that they delight in God's commands rather than finding them burdensome. Joyful obedience to commands that the ungodly find intolerable is evidence of salvation.

※

Psalm 119:73. Your hands have made and fashioned me; give me understanding that I may learn your commandments.

This is the Christian religion in a few words. What faith teaches us to accept is that God gave to each one of us our specific nature (psychological, physical, and spiritual) and station in life. Recognizing that God gives particular aptitudes and knows our attributes better than we know ourselves, we beg God—who remains beyond our full understanding and cannot be approached except by asking for his help—to guide us to our fulfillment. We need him to give us willing minds to learn and obey his commands, which includes everything from his eternal thoughts to our moral obligations.

※

Psalm 119:99. I have more understanding than all my teachers, for your testimonies are my meditation.

God helps people live better than what they have been taught and even to rise above who they themselves are, if they trust in his wisdom. While believers who rely on him from youth are spared many sorrows, even those who repent after suffering divorce, disease, disgrace, or depression have God's promise to bring good to them rather than evil. While some lives are so tangled that sinners beg God to cut sin's cords to begin anew, the Lord patiently unravels and unties knots beyond human repair as he frees his beloved from their sorrows to live in his holy joy.

※

Psalm 119:104. Through your precepts I get understanding; therefore I hate every false way.

Before we censure passages where the psalmist declares his own moral uprightness, we need to reflect on such God-inspired passages. To begin with, they teach that false humility is wrong. When we are upright, we must acknowledge it (while giving God glory for his grace). Second, we must remember that Psalms originally were set to music as corporate confessions. As our own hymn declares: *"The Spirit and the gifts are ours through him who with us sideth."* The hymn composer was not vindicating himself, but acknowledging God's work in calling the faithful to good works (just like the psalmist).

PSALM 119:124-125. Deal with your servant according to your steadfast love, and teach me ... give me understanding, that I may know your testimonies!

Hospitals, sanitariums, and graveyards are filled with those who won't listen. It is necessary to hear what others say about our troubles, whether sorrows or sins. This psalmist trusts in God's love and even begs the Creator to teach him, but he also confesses he must learn God's rules better than he has done—and this from a pious poet rather than a cynic or rebel. Those who ask God for guidance must study wise books just as those who pray for money must seek work. Whoever desires the love and wisdom of God must study biblical laws and teachings.

Psalm 119:151. But you are near, O LORD, and all your commandments are true.

The Psalms are at the heart of biblical religion and this passage summarizes the entire book almost perfectly. It shows two themes that run through the psalms, indeed through prayer itself. First, God seems close to all the psalmist. It is necessary that believers remain convinced that the Lord lives within then even as he guides their thoughts and works his will through their prayers. Second, this interior reality must be consistent with and subordinate to the Lord's work in establishing both earthly and heavenly kingdoms in which his existence is confessed, his word recognized, and his every commandment obeyed.

Psalm 121:7. The LORD will keep you from all evil; he will keep your life.

Faith is complete when we approach the uncertainties of life with a quiet trust that our lives belong to the Maker of heaven and earth. Only then can we face famine, pestilence, and sword (or loneliness, ignominy, and isolation) with full confidence that the Lord who has redeemed us by his own suffering and death remains near. Only then does our faith approach maturity: admitting that evils are real rather than addressing sorrows with glib clichés even as it reminds us that God cares for us in this fallen world and has made us for a reason, an eternal purpose.

Psalm 127:1. Unless the LORD builds the house, those who build it labor in vain. Unless the LORD watches over the city, the watchman stays awake in vain.

This psalm asserts that both public authority and private household are ruled by God's providence. No household is built apart from God's life-giving desire and no state (Jewish kingdom or Gentile empire alike) endures beyond divine allowance. Unless God determines that a man (or woman) and his offspring should be blessed, no plan will prevail against flaws and limits imposed by birth and breeding. Unless God chooses to preserve a government, it cannot remain secure in a world of rebellions and reactions. We must understand in our hearts that God alone provides to mankind both good children and just government.

Psalm 127:4. Like arrows in the hand of a warrior are the children of one's youth.

Often it is forgotten that God ordains both ends and means. Creation was made from absolutely nothing, but now unfolds from what was established—and that in an orderly manner. While the Lord has used miracles to reveal how he stands above his creation, God did not make a world where magic spells break free of the natural order or prayer brings rain from unclouded skies. Likewise, when the Lord blesses the godly with strong sons, it must be understood that he is calling believing parents to raise their children for the purpose of godly strength, physical and moral alike.

PSALM 127:5. Blessed is the man who fills his quiver with them! He shall not be put to shame when he speaks with his enemies in the gate.

Because this psalm is one of my favorite passages, I will not speak of it again since I too often focus on biblical teachings that most please me. Yet, is it not idolatrous to fashion God's Word into my image rather than to teach and live the full breadth of God's revelation while maintaining biblical proportions and priorities? We should neither neglect passages that we judge less important nor dwell on those we ourselves deem most relevant. For this reason, Moses required that Israel assemble annually to hear every single word of God's law read aloud, to include disquieting passages.

PSALM 128:3-4. Your wife will be like a fruitful vine within your house; your children will be like olive shoots around your table. Behold, thus shall the man be blessed who fears the LORD.

He who created heaven and earth knows no division between temporal and spiritual life. Those who fear him, who are conscious to learn and follow his precepts, are blessed in their lives like the first creation. Moral duty leads them to a rich experience of human desires, especially in family life. Conscience protects them from sins that cause decades of remorse, even when the inescapable effects of sin are not clearly perceived. Having lived their lives as God wills, maturation allows such believers to watch their children spread like blackberry shoots—now growing into fruitful canes for many to enjoy.

※

PSALM 130:5. I wait for the LORD, my soul waits, and in his word I hope.

The New Testament warns us not to be drunk with wine, but to be filled with the Spirit. The apostle tells us to sing psalms and make music in our heart to God (exactly as was done several hundred years earlier when this psalmist sang a song from the music deep in his heart). Such spiritual experience is not a mystical leap of faith, but remains in accord with reason and rationality. It is drunks and drug addicts who deny reality, not the writers of hymns and poems using human language and desires to craft precise thoughts into shared songs.

※

PSALM 131:2-3. But I have calmed and quieted my soul, like a weaned child with its mother ...

Believers must learn to accept the difficulties of life just as weaned children have learned not to throw fits and tantrums at pangs of hunger. It is not that our troubles are inconsequential to the Lord, but that the God of Israel (who called a godly nation into existence and defended it amidst heathen empires) can be trusted to be wiser and kinder than an ordinary mother. Even children eventually come to understand that the breast was not denied to starve them, but that tastier and more satisfying food could be offered: food also better for staving off their hunger.

※

PSALM 135:3,6. The Lord is good ... Whatever the LORD pleases, he does, in heaven and on earth, in the seas and all deeps.

Medieval philosophers (and many since) debated the relationship of God's goodness to his power. Here the psalmist affirms the facts of divine goodness and divine power by praising God for both attributes: declaring the idols of the pagans vile compared to God's righteous character and impotent before his unyielding power. That is, the psalmist (unlike Greek philosophers who flourished centuries later) is less concerned with rhetorical consistency than with historical demonstration of God's ability to uphold his laws and protect his people. The Lord didn't send philosophers and poets to inspire his people, but prophets and warriors to save them.

※

PSALM 137:8-9. O daughter of Babylon, doomed to be destroyed, blessed shall he be who repays you with what you have done to us! Blessed shall he be who takes your little ones and dashes them against the rock!

Again—translations matter. Some Bibles almost certainly miss the mark when they replace *blessed* with *happy*, thereby making a profound benediction to God (as the judge of those who oppress Israel) into a facile praise of bloodshed. In like manner, we can call the Greatest Generation *blessed* amidst the wars it fought, but seldom *happy*. The text also acknowledges that God takes human life, sometimes via the hands of evildoers. Even those of us who are passionately anti-communist can discern divine vengeance in the Soviet victory over Nazi Germany, despite the morally repugnant rapes and murders committed by Soviet soldiers.

PSALM 139:1-2. O LORD, you have searched me and known me! You know when I sit down and when I rise up; you discern my thoughts from afar.

It is not enough to center our faith on individual experiences of piety or personal understandings of God's laws and teachings. What matters most is that we begin with a clear understanding of who the Lord is and what he is like. We need to remember his divine nature: that he is eternal, infinite, omniscient, omnipresent, omnipotent, and immutable. We are required to remember that from eternity the Lord has known every detail of our entire life and now governs both us and all creation with infinite wisdom and goodness. His love overrules every mortal power and has no end.

PSALM 139:13-14. For you formed my inward parts; you knitted me together in my mother's womb. I praise you, for I am fearfully and wonderfully made.

Before my parents conceived me (whether by love or lust), I was made in the mind of God. It was he who chose me from the tens of millions of possibilities of that hour and from a $1/10^{2,685,000}$ chance of genetic linkage back to the first couple. If as much as one kiss was spurned in the ancient world or one medieval couple bedded an hour earlier, I would not have been. Unless a zero-odds lottery created the cosmos, God conceived me in his mind from eternity, then knit me in my mother's womb as a life dear to himself.

❧

P<small>SALM</small> *141:2. Let my prayer be counted as incense before you, and the lifting up of my hands as the evening sacrifice!*

The Old Testament blesses the burnt offering: the spotless animal given irrevocably to God through ceasing to be. We must remember there are many types of burnt offerings given to the Lord: money left unearned so we can serve family, entertainment not enjoyed that we might help neighbors, pleasures not taken for the sake of holiness, and careers not vaulted for the sake of integrity. In each of these instances, we offer to God not simply what is, but also what will not be, confessing that Eternal Wisdom alone has the right to choose the perfect path from all possibilities.

❧

P<small>SALM</small> *142:0,7. [A Maskil of David, when he was in the cave.] Bring me out of prison, that I may give thanks to your name!*

It appears that David composed this psalm while he was hiding from Saul in a cave (and spared Saul's life when the latter entered the cave to relieve himself). In like manner, our prayers must be consistent with our moral choices. That is, David prayed from his heart for God's deliverance, then trusted the Lord to save him rather than to take action on his own. Subsequently, the Lord saved David from his foe without David having been morally compromised by any hint whatsoever of treason. Indeed, David even punished the man who sought a reward for having killed Saul.

Psalm 144:1. Blessed be the LORD, my rock, who trains my hands for war, and my fingers for battle.

Some argue that the psalms are imperfect demonstrations of piety, not on par with the Gospels. Such an understanding opens the entire Old Testament to criticism and eventually leaves us with mere fragments of the Gospels remaining as God's authoritative word (and this methodology adopted without any biblical or ecclesiastical authority whatsoever). A more feasible approach would be to assume our sentiments often are mistaken: that both soldiers who pray to survive by killing their enemy and judges who rightly sentence criminals to death do so under divine authority. In that sense, God inspires both lawful killings and helpful sermons.

PSALM 145:1,8. I will extol you, my God and King, and bless your name forever and ever ... The LORD is gracious and merciful, slow to anger and abounding in steadfast love.

It seems almost unbelievable that God would forgive our evil deeds and protect us simply because we have asked him to. What Scripture reveals to us is that our universe at its core is not a matter of energy and mass: reality controlled by physics. Rather, the cosmos is governed by love and what matters most is that we believe God created the world through divine decree of hope, faith, and love spoken into existence. In the same way, even a condemned criminal can hope for God's mercy and speak into existence eternal joy simply by professing faith in Christ.

PSALM 145:4. One generation shall commend your works to another, and shall declare your mighty acts.

It seems (to some) a bit silly to consciously adopt the mindset of Hebrews who lived 3000 years ago. After all, who frames their ethics by the rites of Babylonian priests and dictates of Assyrian kings? But what is striking is how closely the prayers and ideals of ancient Hebrews resemble our own. Indeed, our churches are filled with congregants who sing songs rooted in the Psalms and do so with loud, willing voices. For those who think this ill-considered, we need only point to Athens and Rome—whose philosophies and politics even the most modern among us often emulate.

Psalm 146:8. The LORD opens the eyes of the blind. The LORD lifts up those who are bowed down.

There is a terrible contradiction in nature and history—in life itself. Evil exists and so does good. Blindness afflicts and God heals. Too often we view this inconsistency only from the vantage of our sorrows. While this psalmist does not explain why God allows evil, he does make plain that God permits suffering in context of overcoming it. That is, God delights more in triumph than in avoiding tragedy. We believe the same when we honor the victorious sufferings of Great Britain and Poland (who defeated the Nazi foe) over the unscathed neutrality of countries like Switzerland and Sweden?

※

Psalm 146:9. The LORD watches over the sojourners; he upholds the widow and the fatherless, but the way of the wicked he brings to ruin.

Perhaps 2500 years before Marx argued that history was on the side of the proletariat, this psalmist acknowledged that the Lord controls history not as an inexorable progression of interests or ideals, but as a drama scripted by omnipotent goodness to save the weak and to judge their oppressors. Believers neither trust in nor fear any doctrine of historical change rooted in materialism and unbelief, but hope in the living God who has created and now loves every person from conception to death. Just as God once mustered an army to abolish slavery, so he chips away at child-killing choice.

Psalm 147:7-8. Sing to the LORD with thanksgiving; make melody to our God on the lyre! He covers the heavens with clouds; he prepares rain for the earth; he makes grass grow on the hills.

There have been churches which have condemned the use of musical instruments as distractions. While this sometimes may be necessary as a temporary expedient when musical instruments prevent congregants from singing to God with grateful hearts (as required), this psalmist shows that music is no more an inherent obstacle to religion than nature is. Indeed, just like nature, music is an element of the created order that glorifies God's wisdom and goodness simply by the existence of the natural order that he created. Men need not shape everything into a lesson nor insist that sermons always be preferred above songs.

Psalm 147:14. He makes peace in your borders; he fills you with the finest of the wheat.

Mankind is expected to offer sacrifice to God: the best of what we have and are. We are not to devote our bodies to God only after decades of promiscuity or offer our wealth only after bankruptcy. Rather, our youth and strength are to be offerings. Why? Not only because the Lord made us, but also because we are made like him and should reflect his characteristics. It is the tyrant who serves gruel to captives; God seeds earth with fields of wheat. It is the self-serving prostitute who infects men with loathsome diseases; God creates the purity of brides.

PSALM 149:6-7. Let the high praises of God be in their throats and two-edged swords in their hands, to execute vengeance on the nations and punishments on the peoples.

This psalm would be even more terrible if it were untrue. Though this writer praises crusade in a manner we cannot appreciate amidst wars where religious zealots motivated by death-lust terrorize innocent civilians, the idea of a righteous warrior is better than its alternatives: continued oppression or human indifference. When God seemed to delay his punishment of Holocaust oppression, some lost faith in his goodness and denied his existence. If our grandfathers had not risen to fight fascist tyrants, we would have lost faith in them too. We still honor those who died at Normandy and Okinawa, particularly compassionate soldiers.

PSALM 150:2. Praise him for his mighty deeds; praise him according to his excellent greatness!

Human words—indeed, human thoughts—are incomplete and imperfect. The writer here uses common Hebrew words (translated into English) to suggest how God is powerful beyond limit. While the Hebrew may not reveal the infinite nature of divinity as well as words inherited from Greek and Latin culture, the chosen words do reveal God's personal nature. Philosophical terms such as *omnipotence* or *transcendence* give glimpses into God's unlimited being (the very words make us loathe our insignificance), but render God distant and unfeeling. In contrast, this Hebrew psalm establishes both God's great power and the personal nature of his love.

Made in the USA
Middletown, DE
20 October 2024